Chinese Festivals Cookbook

Stuart Thompson and Angela Dennington with Photography by Zul Mukhida

HODDER
Wayland

An imprint of Hodder Children's Books

FESTIVALS COOKBOOKS

CHRISTIAN FESTIVALS COOKBOOK

HINDU FESTIVALS COOKBOOK

JEWISH FESTIVALS COOKBOOK

CHINESE FESTIVALS COOKBOOK

**NB: Nuts are contained in one of the recipes in this book (see page 28).
Nuts may provoke a dangerous allergic reaction in some people.**

© 2000 White-Thomson Publishing Ltd

Produced for Hodder Wayland by Margot Richardson
23 Hanover Terrace, Brighton, E Sussex, BN2 2SN, UK

Food photography: Zul Mukhida, Chapel Studios, Brighton
Design and illustrations: Tim Mayer
Illustrations: Tim Mayer
Proofreader: Philippa Smith

Published in Great Britain in 2000 by Hodder Wayland,
an imprint of Hodder Children's Books.
This edition published in 2001.

The right of Stuart Thompson and Angela Dennington to be
identified as the authors of this Work has been asserted by them in
accordance with the Copyright, Designs and Patents Act 1988.

Photograph acknowledgements:
Art Directors and TRIP 6, (A Tovy), 22 (P Treanor); The Hutchison
Library 13, (Liba Taylor), 21(Christine Pemberton), 29 (Lesley Nelson);
Impact Photos 4 (Jonathan Pile), 7 (Simon Shepheard), 23 (Christophe Bluntzer);
Wayland Picture Library 6, 14–15 bottom, 15 top (Zul Mukhida).

A catalogue record for this book is available from the British Library.

ISBN 0 7502 3321 4

Printed and bound by G. Canale & C.S.p.A., Turin

Hodder Children's Books
A division of Hodder Headline
338 Euston Road, London NW1 3BH

CONTENTS

Festivals, Food and Firecrackers   4

Chinese New Year Festival   6

Chunjuan   8

Jiaozi   10

The Survival of New Year   13

Dragon Boat Festival   14

Zongzi   16

Charsiu Roast Pork   18

Ludou Tang   20

Other Dragon Boat
Celebrations   21

Mid-Autumn Festival   22

Yuebing   24

Hongshao Dan   26

Tangyuan   28

Other Mid-Autumn Celebrations   29

Further Information   30

Topic Web and Glossary   31

Index   32

Resources   32

Festivals, Food and Firecrackers

China is a huge country. Almost a quarter of the world's people live there. Of the hundreds of festivals in the Chinese calendar, some are celebrated throughout China. The most important are the Chinese New Year festival, the Dragon Boat festival and the Mid-Autumn festival. As well as these famous occasions there used to be hundreds of local festivals.

Both famous and local Chinese festivals are occasions for families, friends or the community to feast and have fun. For children, festivals mean a break from school, and for adults a holiday from work. Festivals are times for enjoyment, and one of the things Chinese people like most is good food. Local festivals give families a welcome excuse to invite friends and relatives to tasty banquets.

By sharing a festive meal, Chinese people show friendship, or the feeling that they belong together.

Some festivals are celebrated at a temple with incense, food and special offerings. This temple is in Hong Kong.

Many Chinese festivals have been celebrated for centuries. At some, families lay out expensive foods. Perfumed smoke from sticks of burning incense respectfully tells gods or ancestors that the food presented is for them. After the gods or ancestors have 'tasted' it, the food offerings provide a feast that the people share. At other festivals, families or communities try to protect themselves from evil or dangerous forces.

Chinese festivals are noisy occasions. There's the noise of many people enjoying food, conversation, and gambling or drinking games. At night, crowds gather to watch open-air operas or puppet shows. Noisiest of all are the firecrackers. The Chinese invented gunpowder long ago, but not for fighting battles. Instead, they made fire-crackers to use on special occasions. The ear-piercing sound of exploding fire-crackers tells the world that there is a celebration, and the noise is believed to scare away ghosts and harmful creatures.

Safety and Hygiene

When cutting with knives, frying, boiling and using the oven, ALWAYS ask an adult to help you.

Food must always be kept clean. Food that gets dirty will not taste good – and can even make people sick.

Always wash your hands before you start cooking.

Do not wipe dirty hands on a towel. Wash your hands first.

If you need to taste something while cooking, use a clean fork or spoon.

Make sure work surfaces are clean and dry. This includes tables, worktops and chopping boards.

CHINESE NEW YEAR FESTIVAL

Exploding firecrackers welcome in the new year and encourage the dragon to dance at these celebrations in Guangxi, China.

Chinese festivals are dated according to a lunar (moon) calendar, based on the phases of the moon. Chinese New Year falls sometime between 16th January and 21st February on the Western solar (sun) calendar. The New Year Festival marks Winter's end and Spring's return. So it is also called Spring Festival. Another farming year will soon start, but first there's time for a festive holiday.

Each family prepares many favourite dishes for its New Year's Eve feast. It is a private meal, for family only. Homes are spring-cleaned, debts repaid, new clothing laid out and baths taken, so that everything and everyone is ready for a clean start to the New Year. Roads and trains are packed as family members who live elsewhere return home. It is the most important time for families to be together.

On New Year's Eve the whole family may spend hours making dumplings or jiaozi (see pages 10–12). Pork is the best-liked meat, but it is good to include chicken (*ji*, pronounced 'jee') since it sounds like the word lucky (*ji*); and fish (*yu*, pronounced 'you') which sounds like the word riches (*yu*). Cutting up food – or anything else – at New Year is believed to cause bad luck, though. The festive food should be 'whole' – like the family.

First, the delicious food is offered to the family's ancestors to show that they are still cared for and remembered. Then, families enjoy the many dishes, staying up late. Next morning, at dawn, screaming blasts of firecrackers noisily announce the New Year. People congratulate their neighbours on surviving to see in another year. It's time to visit friends and relatives. Grandparents give children red packets of 'lucky money'. The holiday atmosphere lasts two more weeks till the Lantern Festival, after which it's back to work and school.

A man dressed as the 'god of money' hands out lucky money envelopes in a festive crowd.

Chunjuan

Preparation time: 20 minutes

Cooking time: 10–20 minutes

Makes: 15–20 spring rolls

Ingredients

250 g mixed vegetables

150 g minced meat

150 g cooked prawns

1 tbsp light soy sauce

1 tsp salt

1 packet of frozen spring roll pastry (approx 11 x 11 cm), thawed

2 tsp plain flour, with a little water added to make a 'glue'

1–1½ litres cooking oil

Equipment

Chopping knife

Wooden spoon

Frying pan (for stir-frying)

Large bowl

Pastry brush

Large pan suitable for deep-frying (or electric deep-fryer)

Paper towel

Baking tray

Chunjuan (pronounced 'chu-en-juan'), or spring rolls, are usually eaten as snacks or part of a meal. Another name for New Year is the Spring Festival, since it marks the start of the Spring season. *Chun* means 'Spring', which is why these rolls are a good food to eat at Chinese New Year.

You can use a variety of vegetables and meat in chunjuan. For vegetables, choose several from cabbage, bean sprouts, bamboo shoots, water chestnuts, mushrooms, leeks, spring onions or carrots. For meat, use pork, beef, chicken or turkey.

1 With an adult's help, finely shred the vegetables so they are all the same size. Put the minced meat in the bowl. Add the soy sauce and salt.

2 Ask an adult to put a little oil in the frying pan. Heat and stir-fry the meat for 30 seconds. Add the vegetables and stir-fry for a further mir

3 Drain off the juices. Empty the mixture into the bowl. Allow to cool. Chop the prawns and mix in well.

4 Lay out a pastry sheet flat, in a diamond shape. Place two tablespoons of filling near the middle. Fold the bottom flap over the filling, tucking the tip of the pastry under. Roll it over once away from you.

5 Keep one hand on the roll, and fold in each end with your other hand. Brush the remaining triangle flap with flour paste to act as a glue. Roll the filling into a tight cylinder.

6 Ask an adult to heat the oil in a deep-fryer or pan. Gently slide in about six rolls. They will float freely. Fry for 4—5 minutes, turning them over once.

7 When the spring rolls are crisp and golden-brown, lift carefully from the oil with a slotted spoon. Put on baking tray lined with paper towel. Place in a heated oven, leaving door open. Deep-fry the remaining spring rolls.

8 Serve hot and crispy. If you like, flavour with soy sauce, a little vinegar, or maybe tomato ketchup.

Jiaozi

These bite-sized dumplings (pronounced 'gee-ow-dze') are often the main Chinese New Year food. Traditional jiaozi are little pouches of dough filled with minced pork, cabbage, ginger and spring onion, but you can experiment with other savoury fillings. Eating dozens of tasty dumplings together is a traditional meal for family gatherings. Everyone, including children, shares in the family teamwork of preparing them.

Preparation time: 25 minutes

Cooking time: 15 minutes per batch of 10-12 dumplings

Makes: about 80 jiaozi

Ingredients

Wrappers

500 g plain white flour

250 ml cold water

Filling

4 sticks celery

1¹/₂ tsp fresh ginger root (optional)

2 spring onions

2 small garlic cloves

250 g minced meat (pork, beef, chicken or turkey)

1 tbsp sesame oil

¹/₂ tsp salt

2 tbsp light soy sauce

Dipping sauce

4 tbsp light soy sauce

4 tbsp vinegar

1 **Wrappers:** mix the flour and water in a bowl and work into a firm, smooth, springy dough. (You may need to add extra flour or water.)

2 Turn the dough on to a lightly floured surface and knead firmly for about 10 minutes until smooth and elastic. Wrap in clingfilm while preparing the filling.

Equipment

2 large bowls

Wooden spoons

Chopping knife

Rolling pin

Large saucepan

2 baking trays

Slotted spoon

3 **Filling:** chop the celery, ginger, spring onions and garlic as fine as possible. Put all the filling ingredients into the mixing bowl. Mix them together well.

4 **Dumpling wrappers:** Divide the dough into four pieces. Keep three pieces under some clingfilm while you work with the other quarter of the dough.

5 Lightly flour the worktop and keep it floured. Knead the dough lightly once more. Roll into a long sausage about 2 cm wide and 30 cm long. Cut into 20 pieces.

6 Flatten a piece of dough with the palm of your hand. Roll from the edge to the centre with the rolling pin. Then turn it 90 degrees and roll again. Keep going until you have a circle of about 8 cm, which is thinner at the edge and thicker in the middle.

7 **Filling dumplings:** Lay out 10–12 dumpling wrappers. Place a heaped teaspoon of the filling in the centre of each circle, keeping well clear of the edges.

8 Carefully lift a wrapper and filling. Cradle it between your thumb and first finger. With your other hand, nip the sides of the wrapper together firmly to make a well-sealed fan-shaped purse.

Jiaozi (continued)

9 Put the dumplings separately on a floured baking tray, ready for cooking. Keep making dumplings till the wrappers and filling are used up.

10 **Cooking dumplings:** Fill the large saucepan half full of water. Ask an adult to bring it to the boil. Using a slotted spoon, put in 10–12 dumplings, one by one, and stir gently, taking care not to puncture the wrappers.

11 Bring the water back to a gentle boil. Boil for 2 minutes. Remove from the heat for 10 minutes. Then bring back to a gentle boil once more. Lift the dumplings out with a slotted spoon.

12 Serve with a separate bowl of dipping sauce. Eat immediately. Repeat until all the dumplings have been cooked – and eaten.

THE SURViVAL OF NeW YeaR

Some years ago, the Chinese government strongly disapproved of traditional festivals, and tried to stop people from celebrating them. They regarded festivals as a waste of time, money and effort. They saw festivals as based on superstitious ideas, and as a way for the rich to cheat the poor.

So the government banned many festivals, or forced people to have simpler and less costly festivals. Instead they created new ones, like Workers' Day (1st May), Children's Day (1st June), National Day (1st October) and Women's Day (8th March).

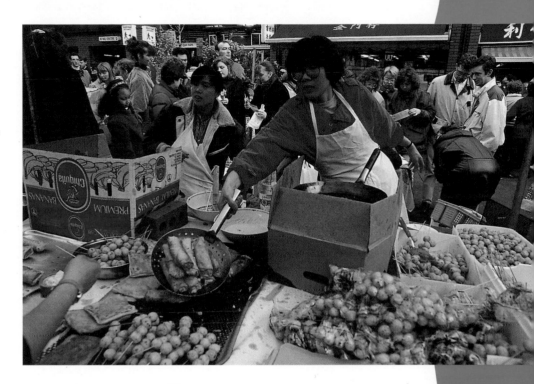

Chinese New Year is celebrated in many different countries where Chinese people live. This food stall in London's Soho serves large spring rolls and other snacks for everyone to enjoy.

But most people did not like these changes. They felt the new holidays were boring: no crowds, no colour, no gambling, no noisy firecrackers – and not even the opportunity to enjoy delicious festive food with family and friends, because the government criticised banquets as wasteful.

Now the government does not interfere so much when people want to celebrate traditional festivals. So once more in China, as for many Chinese people around the world, traditional Chinese New Year is the most important festival for the family to celebrate, usually by enjoying a magnificent meal together.

DRAGON BOAT FESTIVAL

For hundreds of years there have been dragon boat races on the fifth day of the fifth (lunar) month. It is an ancient sports festival held when the summer sun is at its highest in the sky. Another name for the festival is Poet's Day. At school, Chinese children learn the story of why dragon boats are raced on Poet's Day.

The poet Qu Yuan (pronounced 'Chu Yu-en') lived more than 2,000 years ago. He was also an important politician, and was very honest and patriotic. He believed that it was his duty to do everything he could for his country, China. When the corrupt ruler refused to listen to his advice, Qu Yuan felt he had to make the strongest possible complaint. So, in protest, he threw himself into a lake to drown. When local fishermen realized he was drowning, they raced their boats at full speed to save him. They beat drums to frighten off fish, which they feared might eat him. They threw parcels of rice into the water for the fish to feed on instead. But they were too late. The poet's body was never found.

The Dragon Boat Festival is held in Qu Yuan's honour. The boats have a dragon's head carved at the front. Crews race to the beat of their boat's drum.

Zongzi, parcels of leaf-wrapped rice, are the festival's most famous food. They are given as gifts during the fifth month. Barbecue roast pork is a welcome dish at any time, but it tastes best to winning crews! In the summer heat, though, mung bean soup is a good 'cooling' food.

Farmers need summer rain for a good harvest. Perhaps dragon-boat racing encourages rain, since, in Chinese tradition, heavy rain is said to result from dragons fighting in the sky.

Zongzi are often given as gifts during the fifth month.

A traditional dragon boat and crew in southern China. The drum that is beaten for the rowers to follow is the round shape near the front of the boat.

15

Zongzi

Preparation time: 1 hour

Cooking time: 1 hour

Makes: about 10 zongzi

Ingredients

200 g glutinous rice

4 rashers cooked streaky bacon, plus

2 hard-boiled eggs, all chopped and mixed together

Equipment

Large saucepan

Wooden spoon

Large bowl

Medium bowl

10 squares foil, about 20 x 20 cm

20 pieces of string, about 30 cm long

Steamer

These rice parcels, which are usually wrapped in bamboo or lotus leaves, are easily the most famous food for the Dragon Boat Festival. Zongzi (pronounced 'dzong-dze') are usually pyramid shaped, but can be other shapes. The bamboo-leaf wrapping gives a special flavour to the rice. The stuffing inside can be sweet or savoury.

As it is hard to find bamboo leaves, this recipe has been adapted to use aluminium foil to make the parcels.

1 Put the rice in a saucepan. Rinse several times. Drain. Add 300 ml water. With an adult's help, bring it to the boil, stirring often. Simmer until the water is almost all absorbed.

2 Turn the heat very low. Cover with lid. Cook for another 20 minutes. Spoon the rice into a large bowl and allow to cool.

3 Lay out a piece of foil. Add about 3 tablespoons of cooked rice, with some of the bacon and egg filling in the centre.

4 Wrap up the foil parcel, folding in the edges until the rice is completely enclosed.

5 Secure by firmly tying with one piece of string. Use a second piece of string to criss-cross the first.

6 Put 1 litre of water in the saucepan. Put the parcels into the steamer. Ask an adult to bring the water to the boil, then turn the heat down to a simmer. Place the steamer over the hot water and steam the parcels for 1 hour.

7 Carefully unwrap each parcel and serve hot. You can flavour them with some soy sauce.

Charsiu Roast Pork

Preparation time: 1 hour

Cooking time: 1¹/₂ hours

Oven temperature:
200 °C/Gas Mark 6

Ingredients

1–1.5 kg lean pork with a little fat on it, from leg of pork, or pork fillet

2 tbsp hoisin sauce

4 tbsp light soy sauce

4 tbsp sugar

1 teaspoon salt

2 tbsps runny honey

Equipment

Cutting knife

Large bowl

Spoons

Clingfilm

Wire rack (for roasting)

Roasting tin

Small saucepan

Pastry brush

This is a well-known dish from Canton, in southern China. It is often displayed in Cantonese restaurants, hanging from hooks in the window. It can be eaten cold, so is convenient for picnics. Sliced up small, charsiu pork (pronounced 'char-see-oo') is a tasty ingredient in stir-fried or noodle dishes. Children tend to like it best inside steamed buns.

1 Ask an adult to cut the meat into long strips about 4 cm wide. Score along the strip with diagonal cuts every 5 cm or so.

2 Put the hoisin sauce, soy sauce, sugar and salt into a bowl. Mix well. Add the meat pieces. Turn them over to cover them evenly in the marinade.

3 Cover the bowl with clingfilm. Let stand for 2–3 hours, turning the meat over twice to spread the marinade evenly.

4 Ask an adult to preheat the oven. Put the meat pieces on the wire rack with the roasting tin underneath. Add water to the roasting tin until it is 2 cm deep.

5 Roast for about 30 minutes. Then take meat pieces out and dip again in the marinade. Replace them upside-down on the rack. Roast for another 20–30 minutes.

6 Reduce the oven heat if the sauce starts to burn. Check the meat is cooked by sticking a knife into it. If the juice is clear, the meat is cooked. Remove from the oven.

7 Meanwhile, boil up the left-over marinade with the honey, and simmer for about 20 minutes. Brush evenly over the roasted meat while hot.

8 Cut the roasted meat into slices, about 5 mm thick. Serve hot or cold.

Ludou Tang

Preparation time: Overnight

Cooking time: 2¼ hours

Serves: 6

Ingredients

250 g green mung beans

1½ litres water

150 g sugar

Equipment

Large bowl

Large saucepan

This sweet soup made from green mung beans (pronounced 'loo-doe tang'), is popular in southern China. People think that drinking it has a 'cooling' effect in the hot summer.

Chinese people do not usually have a dessert after their meal. Instead they may round off their meal with fresh fruit and Chinese tea. There is a wide variety of cakes, snacks and sweet soups to eat between meals or in the late evening.

1 Rinse the mung beans thoroughly several times.

2 In a large bowl, leave the beans to soak overnight in 1 litre of cold water. Do not drain.

3 Transfer the beans and water to a large saucepan. Add another 500 ml of cold water.

4 With an adult's help, bring to the boil. Then reduce the heat, cover, and simmer for 2 hours. Stir occasionally.

5 Add the sugar. Simmer until the sugar has completely dissolved.

6 Serve hot. But it can be eaten cold, or made into iced lollies.

OTHER DRAGON BOAT CELEBRATIONS

Though the Dragon Boat Festival was banned for some years in China, the boat races have now become a world-wide activity.

Every year since 1976, World Championship International Dragon Boat Races have been held in Hong Kong harbour, with over 100 teams from more than 20 countries taking part. There are Dragon Boat clubs and competitions not only in China, Hong Kong, Taiwan and Singapore, but also in the USA, Canada, Holland, Germany, Britain and Australia.

The dragon boat races held in Hong Kong are a colourful sight, and many people flock to watch them.

On the whole, Dragon Boat Racing has become a popular sport, and, because it is still unusual and quite spectacular to watch, the competitions are often a good way to raise money for charities.

Although zongzi are very popular for this festival, not many people outside China make their own, partly because it is not easy to find the bamboo or lotus leaves for the wrapping. However, many Chinese supermarkets sell uncooked zongzi in May or June, around the time of the festival.

MiD-AUTUMn FESTivaL

Chinese New Year occurs when the spring sun starts to reappear. At the Dragon Boat Festival, the summer sun is at its highest point. At the Mid-Autumn Festival, the sun is weakening. People focus, instead, on the full moon, which is said to be the year's brightest and roundest.

This is a time for families to join together, and for the living to remember their ancestors. Families gather together to 'admire the moon', so this festival is also called the Moon Festival. People eat evening meals out of doors.

Traditionally, by this time, farmers have gathered in their harvest, storing it for the winter ahead. So the Mid-Autumn Festival is also a harvest festival. Many fruits, especially those that are round like the moon, such as melons, are sold in night markets.

During the Mid-Autumn Festival, many people enjoy evening picnics outdoors, by the light of colourful lanterns, in parks or on hillsides.

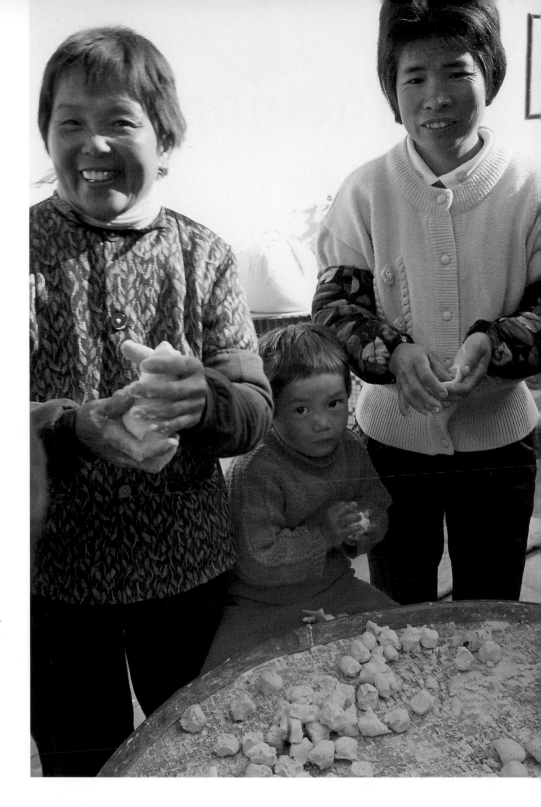

Much of the food enjoyed at this festival is round-shaped, to remind people of the moon. These women are making rice balls similar to those on page 28.

The Moon Festival is supposed to be mostly for women to enjoy, since the moon is said to be female. A famous legend tells how a beautiful princess stole and swallowed pills, which gave her immortality. As a punishment she was turned into a toad, and banished to the moon. Look carefully at the full moon to see if you can spot her shadow.

The festival also marks how, 600 years ago, Chinese people rebelled successfully against Mongolian rulers. Important messages about how and when to rebel were secretly distributed to households by hiding them in moon-cakes (see pages 24–25).

Yuebing

Preparation: 1½ hours

Cooking time: 30 minutes

Oven temperature:
200 °C/Gas Mark 6

Makes: 20

Ingredients

500 g white self-raising flour

3 tbsp vegetable oil

3 eggs

100 g sugar

50 ml water

500 g 'ready to eat'/'no soak' dried figs

20 'ready to eat'/'no soak' dried apricots

1 egg yolk

Equipment

Food processor (optional), OR

   Large mixing bowl

   Wooden spoon

Chopping knife

Baking tray

Fork

Small bowl

Pastry brush

Moon-cakes or yuebing (pronounced 'yu-eh-bing') are the main festive food. They are rich in ingredients and costly to buy. One traditional filling has salted duck egg yolk in a sweet, dark, lotus-seed purée. Slicing through the moon-cake is said to reveal 'the golden moon in a dark sky'. This recipe is adapted here, using puréed figs instead of lotus-seed purée, and a dried apricot for the salted duck egg.

1 Mix the flour, oil, eggs, sugar and water together. (Do this in a bowl, by hand, or ask an adult to use a food processor.) Let the pastry rest in the refrigerator for 30 minutes.

2 With an adult's help, cut the figs into small pieces, then make into a purée. This is easiest in a food processor.

3 Wrap each apricot in fig purée, to make a small ball with the apricot in the centre.

4 Divide the pastry into quarters, then each quarter into 5, to make 20 equal portions. Using the palm of your hand, flatten each pastry portion into a 10 cm circle.

5 Wrap each pastry circle around a ball of fig purée (with an apricot inside it). Press the edges of the pastry together tightly to seal the muffin-shaped cake. Ask an adult to preheat the oven.

6 Turn each cake over so the sealed side is on the bottom. Put on an oiled baking tray. The finished cakes should be about 7 cm in diameter, and 2 cm high. Prick each cake with a fork.

7 Beat the egg yolk, and then brush it lightly on to each cake. Bake in the oven for 30 minutes, or until golden brown.

25

Hongshao Dan

Cooking time: 45 minutes

Serves: 6-8

Ingredients

4-6 eggs

150 ml dark soy sauce

2 cm piece fresh ginger root, peeled and bruised

1 tsp Chinese five-spice powder

1 tbsp sugar

½ tsp salt

100 ml water

Equipment

Small saucepan

Red-dyed boiled eggs or hongshao dan (pronounced 'hong-sha-ow dan') are an appropriate Moon Festival food, as they are round-shaped, and 'red', the Chinese colour for happy events. 'Red-cooking' is a famous type of Chinese cooking in which food is stewed slowly and for a long time in soy sauce. The soy sauce colours the food a dark brownish-red.

1 Ask an adult to help you boil the eggs for 5 minutes. When cooked, rinse the eggs under cold running water to cool them down.

2 When the eggs are cool, remove their shells.

3 Put the soy sauce, ginger, five-spice powder, sugar, salt and water in the saucepan and bring to a simmer. Continue to simmer for 2 minutes to allow the ginger flavour to get into the sauce.

4 With an adult's help, place the peeled eggs carefully into the simmering sauce. Turn each egg so the sauce coats it evenly.

5 Let the eggs cook in the sauce for about half an hour. Turn them over occasionally to get an even coating of the sauce.

6 Serve the eggs with the red-cooked sauce. It tastes very good placed on a bed of plain boiled rice. To eat cold, let the eggs cool in the sauce. Lift them out to eat whole — with your fingers! — or sliced and put in sandwiches.

Tangyuan

These sweet rice balls or tangyuan (pronounced 'tang-yu-en') 'stick together like families should', and are a 'warming' food for the coming winter. They can come in two colours: red or white. They do not always have fillings. In this recipe, a selection of finely ground nuts – hazel, almond, or walnut – is used. You can select the nuts according to your taste.

1 Mix together the ground nuts, butter and 2 tablespoons of sugar. Let the mixture chill in the refrigerator for 30 minutes.

2 Make a dough by mixing the glutinous rice flour with enough water to make a smooth, fairly dry dough. Knead it until it is smooth and springy.

3 Roll into a long sausage shape, about 3 cm diameter and 30 cm long. Cut into 24 pieces. Roll each piece into a ball.

4 Divide the nut mixture into 24 pieces and roll each piece into a little ball.

5 Use your thumb to make a deep dent in each rice ball. Insert a little ball of filling into this dent. Close the dough to cover the filling, and roll into a smooth ball again. Do this for all 24 rice balls.

6 In a saucepan, put the remaining 2 tablespoons of sugar in 1 litre of water. With an adult's help, bring to the boil. Put the rice balls in gently. Cook at medium heat for 5 minutes, or until the balls rise to the surface. Serve hot with the liquid they are cooked in.

OTHER MID-AUTUMN CELEBRATIONS

For about 15 years, until the 1980s, shops in China stopped selling moon-cakes. This was because the Chinese government did not like the celebration of the old festivals. Now there are a huge number of different moon-cakes available in the autumn in all of China's towns and cities. In countries outside China where many Chinese people have settled, moon-cakes are becoming quite a common sight in September or October. In China, the original moon-cakes were probably savoury. They could contain bits of fatty meat as well as other ingredients. Nowadays, in China and elsewhere, most moon-cakes are sweet, though many include a duck's or hen's egg yolk.

In the West, moon-cakes are often brought in from Hong Kong or Taiwan, and sold in attractive tins. They are not cheap – unless you make them yourself!

Except in places where the people are Chinese – such as Hong Kong, Singapore and Taiwan – the Moon Festival is not celebrated so much. Sometimes, though, a Chinese language school or community group will hold a fête using the Mid-Autumn Festival as a focus for a celebration. For both Chinese and non-Chinese people, these days are a convenient excuse to eat lots of tasty Chinese dishes.

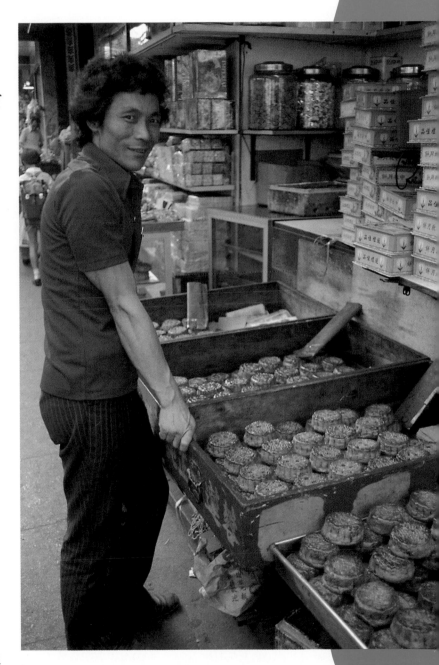

Moon-cakes on sale in Hong Kong, with their decorated tins stacked above.

FURTHER INFORMATION

As well as jiaozi (dumplings) at New Year meals, there is usually a whole fish dish, and round-shaped foods (such as whole eggs or sweet rice balls). The meaning is that families will be 'complete' and 'together' in the year to come.

> When using the recipes contained in this book, children should be supervised by one or more adults at all times. This especially applies when cutting with knives, cooking on a cooker hob and using the oven.

Often there is a sticky New Year cake. The word for cake sounds like the word for 'tall' or 'high', and so eating cake is a way of hoping for success. Some families enjoy a sticky-rice pudding decorated with various dried fruits, called *babaofan*: 'eight jewels rice'.

Another major Chinese festival, which occurs in early April, is called the Clear and Bright (*Qingming*) Festival. Families go to the tombs of their ancestors to show them that they have not been forgotten. They may bring baskets of food and burn spirit money and incense for the ancestors. Some families have a special picnic meal at the graveside. Others return home to share a family banquet as their way of remembering those members of their family who are no longer alive.

EQUIPMENT
The traditional pan for cooking Chinese food is a wok, which is curved like a large bowl. Using a wok with children is not always a good idea as they are easy to tip over during cooking. A thick-bottomed frying pan will be safer and easier to use.

COOKING METHODS
Jiaozi (dumplings): do not be put off by the length of this recipe. This delicious food is surprisingly easy to make, and worth the effort. To make the wrappers easy to handle, keep them well dusted with flour. To seal them successfully, it may help to dip your finger in water and run it around the edge of each wrapper before pinching it together.

Vegetarian dumplings can be made with a vegetable filling such as cabbage and carrots. See Chunjuan (spring rolls).

Zongzi: these rice parcels are traditionally wrapped in bamboo leaves. Dried bamboo leaves can be bought in Chinese supermarkets. To use them, soak first in boiling water for 5 minutes, then drain and cool before wrapping around the filling.

The recipe here gives a savoury filling, but a sweet filling can be used instead: insert a spoonful of canned sweetened chestnut or lotus-seed purée.

INGREDIENTS
NB: Please be aware that nuts are contained in the Sweet Rice Balls (page 28). Nuts may provoke an allergic reaction in some people.

Spring roll pastry Thin squares, available from Chinese shops. It is possible to use Greek filo pastry instead, but it is more brittle, and tends to spit during deep-frying.

Glutinous rice This is a traditional Chinese rice that sticks together when it is cooked.

Glutinous rice flour Made from ground glutinous rice.

Mung beans Small, round, green beans, commonly used in the West for sprouting.

TOPIC WEB

Science
Food and nutrition
Changing materials through heat
Separating/mixing of materials

English
Traditional Chinese stories and legends
Write a poem about a festival

Geography
China: location/features/farming/seasons/weather/culture
Cycles of the moon

Maths
Using and understanding data/measures/fractions
Using measuring instruments

CHINESE FESTIVALS COOKBOOK

History
Chinese migration worldwide
History of China
The story of Qu Yuan

Design and Technology
Construct a box for moon-cakes
Design a paper lantern
Make a model dragon boat

RE
Variety of religions practised in China
Other Chinese festivals

Modern Foreign Languages
Dialects used in China
Learn to say simple phrases/numbers/names of months, etc

GLOSSARY

Ancestors Grandparents, great-grandparents, great-great-grandparents, and so on; the line of family that a person is descended from.

Banned Not allowed, forbidden.

Banquet A special dinner or feast, for many people.

Centuries Hundreds of years.

Congratulate To tell someone 'well done!'

Corrupt Cheating, evil.

Debts What you owe; money you should pay back.

Dragon A legendary animal that breathes fire. It is said that Chinese dragons are powerful creatures that can help human beings.

Immortality Being able to live forever and never die.

Incense A powder that gives off a sweet smell when burned.

Gambling Risking money in the hope of winning more money. If you don't win, then you lose your money.

Government The group of people that rules or leads a country.

Local Belonging to a small area or particular place.

Lunar To do with the moon.

Lunar calendar The Chinese calendar based on the phases of the moon. New moon is the first of the month, and full moon is always on the 15th of the month. There are 29 days in a month. To agree with the Western calendar, in some years there is a 13th month.

Patriotic Loving and caring for one's country.

Politician A person who is part of the government.

Rebelled Protested against the government; refused to obey orders.

Savoury Salty and spiced, not sweet-tasting.

Solar To do with the sun.

Superstitious What you might call people who believe in luck and magic.

Western Belonging to Europe, the USA, Canada, Australia or New Zealand.

INDEX

Page numbers in **bold** refer to photographs

ancestors 5, 7, 22, 31
banquets 4, 13, 31
boats 14–15, **14–15**, 21, **21**
calendar 6, 31
Charsiu Roast Pork 18–19, **18–19**
China 4–5, **6**, 13, 14, 14-**15**, 18, 21, 29
Chinese New Year 4, 6–7, **6**, **7**, 8, 10, 13, **13**, 22, 30
Chunjuan 8–9, **8–9**
Dragon Boat Festival 4, 14–15, **14–15**, 16, 21, **21**, 22
dragons **6**, 15, 31
dumplings 7, 10–11, **10–11**, 30
families 4, 5, 6–7, 10, 13, 22, 28
farmers 15, 22
festivals, other 4, 5, 13
firecrackers 5, **6**, 7, 13
Hong Kong 5, 21, **21**, 29, **29**
Hongshao Dan 26–27, **26–27**
hygiene, rules of 5
Jiaozi 7, 10–12, **10–12**, 30
lucky money 7, **7**, **12**
Ludou Tang 20, **20**
lunar 6, 31
lunar calendar 6, 31
Mid-Autumn (Moon) Festival 4, 22–23, **22**, 26, 29
moon 6, 22–23, 24
moon-cakes 23, 24–25, **24–25**, 29, **29**
mung beans 15, 20, 30
Poet's Day 14
Qu Yuan 14–15
Qingming Festival 30
rice balls **23**, 28, **28**, 30
rice parcels 14, 15, **15** 16–17, **16–17**, 21
safety instructions 5, 30
Spring 6, 8
spring rolls 8–9, **8–9**, **13**
Tangyuan 28, **28**
temple **5**
Yuebing 24–25, **24–25**
Zongzi 15, **15**, 16–17, **16–17**, 21, 30

RESOURCES

Books
Festivals of the World: China by Colin Cheong, (Gareth Stevens, 1997)
A Flavour of China by Amy Shui & Stuart Thompson (Wayland, 1998)
Chinese New Year by Mike Hirst, (Hodder Wayland 1999)
Festivals: Chinese New Year by Sarah Moyse (Wayland, 1996)
Fiesta!: China by Susie Dawson (Franklin Watts, 1997)
Food and Recipes of China by Theresa M Beatty (Powerkids Press, USA, 1999)
Multicultural Stories: Chinese by Saviour Pirotta, (Hodder Children's Books, 2000)

Audio
Teach Me Chinese (A Musical Journey Through the Day) book and cassette (Penton Overseas Inc, 1996, available through www.amazon.co.uk)

Web sites
http://www.edunetconnect.com/cat/soc_cult.html
An informative site, giving information in its 'China Window' about life, culture and festivals, (mainly in Hong Kong). This site links to:
http://www.peacock.tnjc.edu.tw/ADD/TOUR/keep.html
Information on festivals and culture 'keeping faith with the past'.

http://www.chinesesoftware.com
The website of the Chinese Culture Software centre. It sells CD-ROMs containing a wide variety of information.

http://uk.chopstix.net/index.html
A varied site featuring recipes, cultural and festival facts.